GW00587206

To dear Joan
wishing you a very
Happy Birthday
and
many happy returns
with much love
from
Harry + Beryl!
9/7/92

Banjo Paterson's

The POEMS Bush OF

Banjo Paterson's

The POEMS OF Bush

WELDON
PUBLISHING

SYDNEY · HONG KONG · CHICAGO · LONDON

The woodcut on p.22 and the black and white
linocuts throughout the book are by Bruce Goold.

Distributed by Gary Allen Pty Limited
9 Cooper Street, Smithfield, NSW 2164

A Kevin Weldon Production

Published by Weldon Publishing
a division of Kevin Weldon & Associates Pty Limited
372 Eastern Valley Way, Willoughby, NSW 2068, Australia

Edited, designed and produced by Lansdowne Press
First published by J. M. Dent Pty Limited 1987
Reprinted by Weldon Publishing 1991

Poems by A. B. Paterson first published prior to 1 May, 1969 —
Copyright Reserved — Proprietor, Retusa Pty Limited

© Copyright *The Uplift* 1983, Retusa Pty Limited
© Copyright Illustrations individual artists
© Copyright Design Kevin Weldon & Associates Pty Limited

Designed by Elaine Rushbrooke
Produced in Australia by the Publisher
Typeset in Australia by Griffin Press Limited, Adelaide
Printed in Singapore by Kyodo Printing Co. (S'pore) Pte Ltd

National Library of Australia Cataloguing-in-Publication Data

Paterson, A. B. (Andrew Barton), 1864–1941.
Banjo Paterson's poems of the bush.

Includes index.
ISBN 0 86302 129 9

I. Title. II. Title: Poems of the bush.

A821'.2

All rights reserved. Subject to the Copyright Act 1968, no part of this publication
may be reproduced, stored in a retrieval sysem, or transmitted in any form, or by any
means, electronic, mechanical, photocopying, recording, or otherwise, without the
prior written permission of the publisher.

Gumnut design on jacket courtesy Paul Jones and Ascraft Fabrics

Contents

Flying Squirrels

On the rugged water shed
　　At the top of the bridle track
Where years ago, as the old men say,
The splitters went with a bullock dray
　　But never a dray came back.

At the time of the gum tree bloom,
　　When the scent in the air is strong,
And the blossom stirs in the evening breeze,
You may see the squirrels among the trees,
　　Playing the whole night long.

Never a care at all
　　Bothers their simple brains;
You can see them glide in the moonlight dim
From tree to tree and from limb to limb,
　　Little grey aeroplanes.

Each like a dormouse sleeps
　　In the spout of a gum tree old,
A ball of fur with a silver coat;
Each with his tail around his throat
　　For fear of his catching cold.

These are the things he eats,
　　Asking his friends to dine:
Moths and beetles and newborn shoots,
Honey and snacks of the native fruits,
　　And a glass of dew for wine.

Bruce Goold
Waratahs
hand coloured linocut

Song of the Future

'Tis strange that in a land so strong,
So strong and bold in mighty youth,
We have no poet's voice of truth
To sing for us a wondrous song.

Our chiefest singer yet has sung
In wild, sweet notes a passing strain,
All carelessly and sadly flung
To that dull world he thought so vain.

"I care for nothing, good nor bad,
My hopes are gone, my pleasures fled,
I am but sifting sand," he said:
What wonder Gordon's songs were sad!

And yet, not always sad and hard;
In cheerful mood and light of heart
He told the tale of Britomarte,
And wrote the Rhyme of Joyous Guard.

And some have said that Nature's face
To us is always sad; but these
Have never felt the smiling grace
Of waving grass and forest trees
On sunlit plains as wide as seas.

"A land where dull Despair is king
O'er scentless flower and songless bird!"
But we have heard the bellbirds ring
Their silver bells at eventide,
Like fairies on the mountain side,
The sweetest note man ever heard.

The wild thrush lifts a note of mirth;
The bronzewing pigeons call and coo
Beside their nests the long day through;
The magpie warbles clear and strong
A joyous, glad, thanksgiving song,
For all God's mercies upon earth.

8

Fred Williams 1927–1982 Australian
Landscape
gouache, 55.8 × 75.6 cm
Elder Bequest 1969
collection: Art Gallery of South Australia

And many voices such as these
Are joyful sounds for those to tell,
Who know the Bush and love it well,
With all its hidden mysteries.

We cannot love the restless sea,
That rolls and tosses to and fro
Like some fierce creature in its glee;
For human weal or human woe
It has no touch of sympathy.

For us the bush is never sad:
Its myriad voices whisper low,
In tones the bushmen only know,
Its sympathy and welcome glad.

For us the roving breezes bring
From many a blossom-tufted tree —
Where wild bees murmur dreamily —
The honey-laden breath of Spring.

We have no tales of other days,
No bygone history to tell;
Our tales are told where campfires blaze
At midnight, when the solemn hush
Of that vast wonderland, the Bush,
Hath laid on every heart its spell.

Although we have no songs of strife,
Of bloodshed reddening the land,
We yet may find achievements grand
Within the bushman's quiet life.

Lift ye your faces to the sky
Ye far blue mountains of the west,
Who lie so peacefully at rest
Enshrouded in a haze of blue;
'Tis hard to feel that years went by
Before the pioneers broke through
Your rocky heights and walls of stone,
And made your secrets all their own.

For years the fertile western plains
Were hid behind your sullen walls,
Your cliffs and crags and waterfalls
All weatherworn with tropic rains.

Between the mountains and the sea,
Like Israelites with staff in hand,
The people waited restlessly:
They looked towards the mountains old
And saw the sunsets come and go
With gorgeous golden afterglow,
That made the west a fairyland,
And marvelled what that west might be
Of which such wondrous tales were told.

For tales were told of inland seas
Like sullen oceans, salt and dead,
And sandy deserts, white and wan,
Where never trod the foot of man,
Nor bird went winging overhead,
Nor ever stirred a gracious breeze
To wake the silence with its breath —
A land of loneliness and death.

At length the hardy pioneers
By rock and crag found out the way,
And woke with voices of today,
A silence kept for years and years.

Upon the western slope they stood
And saw — a wide expanse of plain
As far as eye could stretch or see
Go rolling westward endlessly.
The native grasses, tall as grain,
Were waved and rippled in the breeze;
From boughs of blossom laden trees
The parrots answered back again.
They saw the land that it was good,
A land of fatness all untrod,
And gave their silent thanks to God.

The way is won! The way is won!
And straightway from the barren coast
There came a westward-marching host,
That aye and ever onward prest
With eager faces to the west,
Along the pathway of the sun.

The mountains saw them marching by:
They faced the all-consuming drought,
They would not rest in settled land:
But, taking each his life in hand,
Their faces ever westward bent
Beyond the farthest settlement,
Responding to the challenge cry
Of "better country further out".

And lo a miracle! the land
But yesterday was all unknown,
The wild man's boomerang was thrown
Where now great busy cities stand.

It was not much, you say, that these
Should win their way where none withstood;
In sooth there was not much of blood
No war was fought between the seas.

It was not much! but we who know
The strange capricious land they trod —
At times a stricken, parching sod,
At times with raging floods beset —
Through which they found their lonely way,
Are quite content that you should say
It was not much, while we can feel
That nothing in the ages old,
In song or story written yet
On Grecian urn or Roman arch,
Though it should ring with clash of steel,
Could braver histories unfold
Than this bush story, yet untold —
The story of their westward march.

12

But times are changed, and changes rung
From old to new — the olden days,
The old bush life and all its ways
Are passing from us all unsung.

The freedom, and the hopeful sense
Of toil that brought due recompense,
Of room for all, has passed away,
And lies forgotten with the dead.
Within our streets men cry for bread
In cities built but yesterday.

About us stretches wealth of land,
A boundless wealth of virgin soil
As yet unfruitful and untilled!
Our willing workmen, strong and skilled
Within our cities idle stand,
And cry aloud for leave to toil.

The stunted children come and go
In squalid lanes and alleys black;
We follow but the beaten track
Of other nations, and we grow
In wealth for some — for many, woe.

And it may be that we who live
In this new land apart, beyond
The hard old world grown fierce and fond
And bound by precedent and bond,
May read the riddle right and give
New hope to those who dimly see
That all things may be yet for good,
And teach the world at length to be
One vast united brotherhood.

So may it be, and he who sings
In accents hopeful, clear, and strong,
The glories which that future brings
Shall sing, indeed, a wondrous song.

The Weather Prophet

"'Ow can it rain," the old man said, "with things the way they are?
You've got to learn off ant and bee, and jackass and galah;
And no man never saw it rain, for fifty years at least,
Not when the blessed parakeets are flyin' to the east!"

The weeks went by, the squatter wrote to tell his bank the news.
"It's still as dry as dust," he said, "I'm feeding all the ewes;
The overdraft would sink a ship, but make your mind at rest,
It's all right now, the parakeets are flyin' to the west".

Bruce Goold
Cockatoo
hand coloured linocut

14

W. Blamire Young 1862–1935
Dry Weather. 1912
watercolour, 56 × 76.8 cm
Art Gallery of New South Wales

Black Harry's Team

No soft-skinned Durham steers are they,
    No Devons plump and red,
But brindled, black, and iron-grey
    That mark the mountain-bred;
For mountain-bred and mountain-broke,
    With sullen eyes agleam,
No stranger's hand could put a yoke
    On old Black Harry's team.

Pull out, pull out, at break of morn
    The creeks are running white,
And Tiger, Spot, and Snailey-horn
    Must bend their bows by night;
And axles, wheels and flooring boards
    Are swept with flying spray
As, shoulder-deep, through mountain fords
    The leaders feel their way.

He needs no sign of cross or kirn
    To guide him as he goes,
For every twist and every turn
    That old black leader knows.
Up mountains steep they heave and strain
    Where never wheel has rolled,
And what the toiling leaders gain
    The body bullocks hold.

Where eaglehawks their eyries make,
    On sidelings steep and blind,
He rigs the gear old Nuttharul Inaks
    A tree tied on behind.
Up mountains, straining to the full,
    Each poler plays his part —
The sullen, stubborn, bullock pull
    That breaks a horse's heart.

16

Beyond the furthest bridle track
  His wheels have blazed the way;
The forest giants, burnt and black,
  Are earmarked by his dray.
Through belts of scrub where messmates grow
  His juggernaut has rolled,
For stumps and saplings have to go
  When Harry's team takes hold.

On easy grade and rubber tyre
  The tourist car goes through;
They halt a moment to admire
  The far-flung mountain view.
The tourist folk would be amazed
  If they could get to know
They take the track Black Harry blazed
  A hundred years ago.

Australian Scenery

The Mountains

A land of sombre, silent hills, where mountain cattle go
By twisted tracks, on sidelings steep, where giant gum trees grow
And the wind replies, in the river oaks, to the song of the stream below.

A land where the hills keep watch and ward, silent and wide awake
As those who sit by a dead campfire, and wait for the dawn to break,
Or those who watched by the Holy Cross for the dead Redeemer's sake.

A land where silence lies so deep that sound itself is dead
And a gaunt grey bird, like a homeless soul, drifts, noiseless, overhead
And the world's great story is left untold, and the message is left unsaid.

The Plains

A land, as far as the eye can see, where the waving grasses grow
Or the plains are blackened and burnt and bare, where the false mirages go
Like shifting symbols of hope deferred — land where you never know.

Land of plenty or land of want, where the grey Companions dance,
Feast or famine, or hope or fear, and in all things land of chance,
Where Nature pampers or Nature slays, in her ruthless, red, romance.

And we catch a sound of a fairy's song, as the wind goes whipping by,
Or a scent like incense drifts along from the herbage ripe and dry
— Or the dust storms dance on their ballroom floor, where the bones of the cattle lie.

Arthur Streeton 1867–1943 Australian
The Valley from Kennon's
oil on canvas, 69.2 × 86.6 cm
Felton Bequest 1925
National Gallery of Victoria, Melbourne

Sunrise on the Coast

Grey dawn on the sandhills — the night wind has drifted
　　All night from the rollers a scent of the sea;
With the dawn the grey fog his battalions has lifted,
　　At the scent of the morning they scatter and flee.

Like mariners calling the roll of their number
　　The sea fowl put out to the infinite deep.
And far overhead — sinking softly to slumber —
　　Worn out by their watching, the stars fall asleep.

To eastward where resteth the dome of the skies on
　　The sea line stirs softly the curtain of night;
And far from behind the enshrouded horizon
　　Comes the voice of a God saying, "Let there be light."

And lo, there is light! Evanescent and tender,
　　It glows ruby-red where 'twas now ashen grey;
And purple and scarlet and gold in its splendour —
　　Behold, 'tis that marvel, the birth of a day!

William Lister Lister
Beach Scene
watercolour and pencil, 56 × 96.5 cm
collection: Australian National Gallery, Canberra

At the Melting of the Snow

There's a sunny southern land,
　　And it's there that I would be
Where the big hills stand,
　　In the south countrie!
When the wattles bloom again,
　　Then it's time for us to go
To the old Monaro country
　　At the melting of the snow.

To the east or to the west,
　　Or wherever you may be,
You will find no place
　　Like the south countrie.
For the skies are blue above,
　　And the grass is green below,
In the old Monaro country
　　At the melting of the snow.

Now the team is in the plough,
　　And the thrushes start to sing,
And the pigeons on the bough
　　Are rejoicing at the spring.
So come my comrades all,
　　Let us saddle up and go
To the old Monaro country
　　At the melting of the snow.

J. J. Hilder 1881–1916
Ploughing. 1910
watercolour, 22.9 × 29.1 cm
Bequest of Dr. & Mrs. Sinclair Gillies 1952
Art Gallery of New South Wales

The Old Australian Ways

The London lights are far abeam
   Behind a bank of cloud,
Along the shore the gas lights gleam,
   The gale is piping loud;
And down the Channel, groping blind,
   We drove her through the haze
Towards the land we left behind —
The good old land of "never mind",
   And old Australian ways.

The narrow ways of English folk
   Are not for such as we;
They bear the long-accustomed yoke
   Of staid conservancy:
But all our roads are new and strange
   And through our blood there runs
The vagabonding love of change
That drove us westward of the range
   And westward of the suns.

The city folk go to and fro
   Behind a prison's bars,
They never feel the breezes blow
   And never see the stars;
They never hear in blossomed trees
   The music low and sweet
Of wild birds making melodies,
Nor catch the little laughing breeze
   That whispers in the wheat.

Our fathers came of roving stock
   That could not fixed abide:
And we have followed field and flock
   Since e'er we learnt to ride;
By miner's camp and shearing shed,
   In land of heat and drought,
We followed where our fortunes led,
With fortune always on ahead
   And always further out.

Bruce Goold
Wattle
hand coloured linocut

The wind is in the barley grass,
    The wattles are in bloom;
The breezes greet us as they pass
    With honey-sweet perfume;
The parakeets go screaming by
    With flash of golden wing,
And from the swamp the wild ducks cry
Their long-drawn note of revelry,
    Rejoicing at the spring.

So throw the weary pen aside
    And let the papers rest,
For we must saddle up and ride
    Towards the blue hill's breast;
And we must travel far and fast
    Across their rugged maze,
To find the Spring of Youth at last,
And call back from the buried past
    The old Australian ways.

When Clancy took the drover's track
    In years of long ago,
He drifted to the outer back
    Beyond the Overflow;
By rolling plain and rocky shelf,
    With stockwhip in his hand,
He reached at last, oh lucky elf,
The Town of Come-and-Help-Yourself
    In Rough-and-Ready Land

And if it be that you would know
    The tracks he used to ride,
Then you must saddle up and go
    Beyond the Queensland side —
Beyond the reach of rule or law,
    To ride the long day through,
In Nature's homestead — filled with awe:
You then might see what Clancy saw
    And know what Clancy knew.

26

A Singer of the Bush

There is waving of grass in the breeze
   And a song in the air,
And a murmur of myriad bees
   That toil everywhere.
There is scent in the blossom and bough,
   And the breath of the spring
Is as soft as a kiss on a brow —
   And springtime I sing.

There is drought on the land, and the stock
   Tumble down in their tracks
Or follow — a tottering flock —
   The scrub-cutter's axe.
While ever a creature survives
   The axes shall swing;
We are fighting with fate for their lives —
   And the combat I sing.

By *the* Grey Gulf-water

Far to the northward there lies a land,
  A wonderful land that the winds blow over,
And none may fathom nor understand
  The charm it holds for the restless rover;
A great grey chaos — a land half made,
  Where endless space is and no life stirreth;
And the soul of a man will recoil afraid
  From the sphinx-like visage that Nature weareth.
But old Dame Nature, though scornful, craves
  Her dole of death and her share of slaughter;
Many indeed are the nameless graves
  Where her victims sleep by the Grey Gulf-water.

Slowly and slowly those grey streams glide,
  Drifting along with a languid motion,
Lapping the reed beds on either side,
  Wending their way to the Northern Ocean.
Grey are the plains where the emus pass
  Silent and slow, with their staid demeanour;
Over the dead men's graves the grass
  Maybe is waving a trifle greener.
Down in the world where men toil and spin
  Dame Nature smiles as man's hand has taught her;
Only the dead men her smiles can win
  In the great lone land by the Grey Gulf-water.

For the strength of man is an insect's strength,
  In the face of that mighty plain and river,
And the life of a man is a moment's length
  To the life of the stream that will run for ever.
And so it cometh they take no part
  In small-world worries; each hardy rover
Rideth abroad and is light of heart,
  With the plains around and the blue sky over.
And up in the heavens the brown lark sings
  The songs that the strange wild land has taught her;
Full of thanksgiving her sweet song rings —
  And I wish I were back by the Grey Gulf-water.

Penleigh Boyd 1890–1923
The River. 1919
watercolour, 45.3 × 53.7 cm
Art Gallery of New South Wales

With the Cattle

The drought is down on field and flock,
    The river bed is dry;
And we shift the starving stock
    Before the cattle die.
We muster up with weary hearts
    At breaking of the day,
And turn our heads to foreign parts,
    To take the stock away.
      And it's hunt 'em up and dog 'em,
      And it's get the whip and flog 'em,
For it's weary work is droving when they're dying every day;
      By stock routes bare and eaten,
      On dusty roads and beaten,
With half a chance to save their lives we take the stock away.

We cannot use the whip for shame
    On beasts that crawl along;
We have to drop the weak and lame,
    And try to save the strong;
The wrath of God is on the track,
    The drought fiend holds his sway,
With blows and cries and stockwhip crack
    We take the stock away.
      As they fall we leave them lying,
      With the crows to watch them dying,
Grim sextons of the Overland that fasten on their prey;
      By the fiery dust storm drifting,
      And the mocking mirage shifting,
In heat and drought and hopeless pain we take the stock away.

In dull despair the days go by
    With never hope of change,
But every stage we draw more nigh
    Towards the mountain range;
And some may live to climb the pass,
    And reach the great plateau,
And revel in the mountain grass,
    By streamlets fed with snow.

Julian Ashton 1851–1942
A Waterhole on the Hawkesbury River. 1885
oil on canvas, 59 × 95 cm
Art Gallery of New South Wales

As the mountain wind is blowing
It starts the cattle lowing,
And calling to each other down the dusty long array;
And there speaks a grizzled drover:
"Well, thank God, the worst is over,
The creatures smell the mountain grass that's twenty miles away."

They press towards the mountain grass,
   They look with eager eyes
Along the rugged stony pass,
   That slopes towards the skies;
Their feet may bleed from rocks and stones,
   But though the blood-drop starts,
They struggle on with stifled groans,
   For hope is in their hearts.
      And the cattle that are leading,
      Though their feet are worn and bleeding,
Are breaking to a kind of run — pull up, and let them go!
      For the mountain wind is blowing,
      And the mountain grass is growing,
They settle down by running streams ice-cold with melted snow.

The days are done of heat and drought
   Upon the stricken plain;
The wind has shifted right about,
   And brought the welcome rain;
The river runs with sullen roar,
   All flecked with yellow foam,
And we must take the road once more,
   To bring the cattle home.
      And it's "Lads! we'll raise a chorus,
      There's a pleasant trip before us."
And the horses bound beneath us as we start them down the track;
      And the drovers canter, singing,
      Through the sweet green grasses springing,
Towards the far-off mountain land, to bring the cattle back.

Are these the beasts we brought away
   That move so lively now?
They scatter off like flying spray
   Across the mountain's brow;
And dashing down the rugged range
   We hear the stockwhip crack,
Good faith, it is a welcome change

To bring such cattle back.
   And it's "Steady down the lead there!"
   And it's "Let 'em stop and feed there!"
For they're wild as mountain eagles and their sides are all afoam;
    But they're settling down already,
    And they'll travel nice and steady,
With cheery call and jest and song we fetch the cattle home.

We have to watch them close at night
  For fear they'll make a rush,
And break away in headlong flight
  Across the open bush;
And by the campfire's cheery blaze,
  With mellow voice and strong,
We hear the lonely watchman raise
  The Overlander's song:
    "Oh! it's when we're done with roving,
    With the camping and the droving,
It's homeward down the Bland we'll go, and never more we'll roam;"
    While the stars shine out above us,
    Like the eyes of those who love us —
The eyes of those who watch and wait to greet the cattle home.

The plains are all awave with grass,
  The skies are deepest blue;
And leisurely the cattle pass
  And feed the long day through;
But when we sight the station gate,
  We make the stockwhips crack,
A welcome sound to those who wait
  To greet the cattle back:
    And through the twilight falling
    We hear their voices calling,
As the cattle splash across the ford and churn it into foam;
    And the children run to meet us,
    And our wives and sweethearts greet us,
Their heroes from the Overland who brought the cattle home.

The Wind's Message

There came a whisper down the Bland* between the dawn and dark,
Above the tossing of the pines, above the river's flow;
It stirred the boughs of giant gums and stalwart ironbark;
It drifted where the wild ducks played amid the swamps below;
It brought a breath of mountain air from off the hills of pine,
A scent of eucalyptus trees in honey-laden bloom;
And drifting, drifting far away along the southern line
It caught from leaf and grass and fern a subtle strange perfume.

It reached the toiling city folk, but few there were that heard —
The rattle of their busy life had choked the whisper down;
And some but caught a fresh-blown breeze with scent of pine that stirred
A thought of blue hills far away beyond the smoky town;
And others heard the whisper pass, but could not understand
The magic of the breeze's breath that set their hearts aglow,
Nor how the roving wind could bring across the Overland
A sound of voices silent now and songs of long ago.

But some that heard the whisper clear were filled with vague unrest;
The breeze had brought its message home, they could not fixed abide;
Their fancies wandered all the day towards the blue hills' breast,
Towards the sunny slopes that lie along the riverside,
The mighty rolling western plains are very fair to see,
Where waving to the passing breeze the silver myalls stand,
But fairer are the giant hills, all rugged though they be,
From which the two great rivers rise that run along the Bland.

Oh! rocky range and rugged spur and river running clear,
[illegible line]
Though we, your sons, are far away, we sometimes seem to hear
The message that the breezes bring to call the wanderers home.
The mountain peaks are white with snow that feeds a thousand rills,
Along the river banks the maize grows tall on virgin land,
And we shall live to see once more those sunny southern hills,
And strike once more the bridle track that leads along the Bland.

* *The Bland*   A county in the southern districts of New South Wales.

Sydney Long 1878–1955 Australian
The Hawkesbury at Wiseman's Point
oil on canvas, 64 × 76.8 cm
Felton Bequest 1931
National Gallery of Victoria, Melbourne

The Travelling Post Office

The roving breezes come and go, the reed beds sweep and sway,
The sleepy river murmurs low, and loiters on its way,
It is the land of lots o' time along the Castlereagh.

The old man's son had left the farm, he found it dull and slow,
He drifted to the great north-west where all the rovers go.
"He's gone so long," the old man said, "he's dropped right out of mind,
But if you'd write a line to him I'd take it very kind;
He's shearing here and fencing there, a kind of waif and stray,
He's droving now with Conroy's sheep along the Castlereagh.
The sheep are travelling for the grass, and travelling very slow;
They may be at Mundooran now, or past the Overflow,
Or tramping down the black soil flats across by Waddiwong,
But all those little country towns would send the letter wrong,
The mailman, if he's extra tired, would pass them in his sleep,
It's safest to address the note to 'Care of Conroy's sheep'.
For five and twenty thousand head can scarcely go astray,
You write to 'Care of Conroy's sheep along the Castlereagh'."

By rock and ridge and riverside the western mail has gone,
Across the great Blue Mountain Range to take that letter on.
A moment on the topmost grade while open fire doors glare,
She pauses like a living thing to breathe the mountain air,
Then launches down the other side across the plains away
To bear that note to "Conroy's sheep along the Castlereagh".

And now by coach and mailman's bag it goes from town to town,
And Conroy's Gap and Conroy's Creek have marked it "further down"
Beneath a sky of deepest blue where never cloud abides,
A speck upon the waste of plain the lonely mailman rides.
Where fierce hot winds have set the pine and myall boughs asweep
He hails the shearers passing by for news of Conroy's sheep.
By big lagoons where wildfowl play and crested pigeons flock,
By campfires where the drovers ride around their restless stock,
And past the teamster toiling down to fetch the wool away
My letter chases Conroy's sheep along the Castlereagh.

Albert Hanson 1866–1914
Australian Sheep Country. 1908
watercolour, 59.5 × 93 cm
Art Gallery of New South Wales

Black Swans

As I lie at rest on a patch of clover
In the western park when the day is done,
I watch as the wild black swans fly over
With their phalanx turned to the sinking sun;
And I hear the clang of their leader crying
To a lagging mate in the rearward flying,
And they fade away in the darkness dying,
Where the stars are mustering one by one.

Oh! ye wild black swans, 'twere a world of wonder
For a while to join in your westward flight,
With the stars above and the dim earth under,
Through the cooling air of the glorious night.
As we swept along on our pinions winging,
We should catch the chime of a church-bell ringing,
Or the distant note of a torrent singing,
Or the far-off flash of a station light.

From the northern lakes with the reeds and rushes,
Where the hills are clothed with a purple haze,
Where the bellbirds chime and the songs of thrushes
Make sweet music in the jungle maze,
They will hold their course to the westward ever,
Till they reach the banks of the old grey river,
Where the waters wash, and the reed beds quiver
In the burning heat of the summer days.

Oh! ye strange wild birds, will ye bear a greeting
To the folk that live in that western land?
Then for every sweep of your pinions beating,
Ye shall bear a wish to the sunburnt band,
To the stalwart men who are stoutly fighting
With the heat and drought and dust storm smiting,
Yet whose life somehow has a strange inviting,
When once to the work they have put their hand.

Margaret Preston
Lake of Swans. 1935
linocut
collection: S. H. Ervin Gallery, National Trust of Australia (NSW)

Facing it yet! Oh, my friend stout-hearted,
What does it matter for rain or shine,
For the hopes deferred and the gain departed?
Nothing could conquer that heart of thine.
And thy health and strength are beyond confessing
As the only joys that are worth possessing.
May the days to come be as rich in blessing
As the days we spent in the auld lang syne.

I would fain go back to the old grey river,
To the old bush days when our hearts were light,
But, alas! those days they have fled for ever,
They are like the swans that have swept from sight.
And I know full well that the strangers' faces
Would meet us now in our dearest places;
For our day is dead and has left no traces
But the thoughts that live in my mind tonight.

There are folk long dead, and our hearts would sicken —
We would grieve for them with a bitter pain,
If the past could live and the dead could quicken,
We then might turn to that life again.
But on lonely nights we would hear them calling,
We should hear their steps on the pathways falling,
We should loathe the life with a hate appalling
In our lonely rides by the ridge and plain.

In the silent park is a scent of clover,
And the distant roar of the town is dead,
And I hear once more as the swans fly over
Their far-off clamour from overhead.
They are flying west by their instinct guided,
And for man likewise is his fate decided,
And griefs apportioned and joys divided
By a mighty power with a purpose dread.

Buffalo Country

Out where the grey streams glide,
Sullen and deep and slow,
And the alligators slide
From the mud to the depths below
Or drift on the stream like a floating death,
Where the fever comes on the south wind's breath,
There is the buffalo.

Out on the big lagoons,
Where the Regia lilies float,
And the Nankin heron croons
With a deep ill-omened note,
In the ooze and the mud of the swamps below
Lazily wallows the buffalo,
Buried to nose and throat.

From the hunter's gun he hides
In the jungles dark and damp,
Where the slinking dingo glides
And the flying foxes camp;
Hanging like myriad fiends in line
Where the trailing creepers twist and twine
And the sun is a sluggish lamp.

On the edge of the rolling plains
Where the coarse cane grasses swell,
Lush with the tropic rains
In the noontide's drowsy spell,
Slowly the buffalo grazes through
Where the brolgas dance, and the jabiru
Stands like a sentinel.

All that the world can know
Of the wild and the weird is here,
Where the black men come and go
With their boomerang and spear,
And the wild duck darken the evening sky
As they fly to their nests in the reed beds high
When the tropic night is near.

A Mountain Station

I bought a run a while ago,
   On country rough and ridgy,
Where wallaroos and wombats grow —
   The Upper Murrumbidgee.
The grass is rather scant, it's true,
   But this a fair exchange is,
The sheep can see a lovely view
   By climbing up the ranges.

And "She-oak Flat" 's the station's name,
   I'm not surprised at that, sirs:
The oaks were there before I came,
   And I supplied the flat, sirs.
A man would wonder how it's done,
   The stock so soon decreases —
They sometimes tumble off the run
   And break themselves to pieces.

I've tried to make expenses meet,
   But wasted all my labours,
The sheep the dingoes didn't eat
   Were stolen by the neighbours.
They stole my pears — my native pears —
   Those thrice-convicted felons,
And ravished from me unawares
   My crop of paddymelons.

And sometimes under sunny skies,
   Without an explanation,
The Murrumbidgee used to rise
   And overflow the station.
But this was caused (as now I know)
   When summer sunshine glowing
Had melted all Kiandra's snow
   And set the river going.

Nicholas Chevalier 1828–1902
A Victorian Homestead. c. 1860
oil on cardboard, 39.4 × 58.4 cm
Bequest of Mrs. Nicholas Chevalier 1919
Art Gallery of New South Wales

And in the news, perhaps you read:
    "Stock passings. Puckawidgee,
Fat cattle: Seven hundred head
    Swept down the Murrumbidgee;
Their destination's quite obscure,
    But, somehow, there's a notion,
Unless the river falls, they're sure
    To reach the Southern Ocean."

So after that I'll give it best;
    No more with Fate I'll battle.
I'll let the river take the rest,
    For those were all my cattle.
And with one comprehensive curse
    I close my brief narration,
And advertise it in my verse —
    "For Sale! A Mountain Station".

The Daylight is Dying

The daylight is dying
    Away in the west,
The wild birds are flying
    In silence to rest;
In leafage and frondage
    Where shadows are deep,
They pass to its bondage —
    The kingdom of sleep.
And watched in their sleeping
    By stars in the height,
They rest in your keeping,
    Oh, wonderful night.

When night doth her glories
    Of starshine unfold,
'Tis then that the stories
    Of bushland are told.
Unnumbered I hold them
    In memories bright,
But who could unfold them,
    Or read them aright?
Beyond all denials
    The stars in their glories
The breeze in the myalls
    Are part of these stories.
The waving of grasses,
    The song of the river
That sings as it passes
    For ever and ever,
The hobble chains rattle,
    The calling of birds,
The lowing of cattle
    Must blend with the words.

Without these, indeed, you
   Would find it ere long,
As though I should read you
   The words of a song
That lamely would linger
   When lacking the rune,
The voice of the singer,
   The lilt of the tune.

But, as one half-hearing
   An old-time refrain,
With memory clearing,
   Recalls it again,
These tales, roughly wrought of
   The bush and its ways,
May call back a thought of
   The wandering days,
And, blending with each
   In the mem'ries that throng,
There haply shall reach
   You some echo of song.

J. J. Hilder 1881–1916
At Close of Day. 1914
watercolour, 56.8 × 65.5 cm
Art Gallery of New South Wales

Clancy of The Overflow

I had written him a letter which I had, for want of better
  Knowledge, sent to where I met him down the Lachlan, years ago,
He was shearing when I knew him, so I sent the letter to him,
  Just "on spec", addressed as follows: "Clancy, of The Overflow".

And an answer came directed in a writing unexpected,
  (And I think the same was written with a thumbnail dipped in tar)
'Twas his shearing mate who wrote it, and *verbatim* I will quote it:
  "Clancy's gone to Queensland droving, and we don't know where he are."

In my wild erratic fancy visions come to me of Clancy
  Gone a-droving "down the Cooper" where the western drovers go;
As the stock are slowly stringing, Clancy rides behind them singing,
  For the drover's life has pleasures that the townsfolk never know.

And the bush hath friends to meet him, and their kindly voices greet him
  In the murmur of the breezes and the river on its bars,
And he sees the vision splendid of the sunlit plains extended,
  And at night the wondrous glory of the everlasting stars.

I am sitting in my dingy little office, where a stingy
  Ray of sunlight struggles feebly down between the houses tall,
And the foetid air and gritty of the dusty, dirty city
  Through the open window floating, spreads its foulness over all.

And in place of lowing cattle, I can hear the fiendish rattle
  Of the tramways and the buses making hurry down the street,
And the language uninviting of the gutter children fighting,
  Comes fitfully and faintly through the ceaseless tramp of feet.

And the hurrying people daunt me, and their pallid faces haunt me
  As they shoulder one another in their rush and nervous haste,
With their eager eyes and greedy, and their stunted forms and weedy,
  For townsfolk have no time to grow, they have no time to waste.

And I somehow rather fancy that I'd like to change with Clancy,
  Like to take a turn at droving where the seasons come and go,
While he faced the round eternal of the cashbook and the journal —
  But I doubt he'd suit the office, Clancy, of "The Overflow".

W. Blamire Young
Shadows of a Great City c.1930
watercolour
collection: S. H. Ervin Gallery
gift of the Friends of the S. H. Ervin Gallery

On Kiley's Run

The roving breezes come and go
  On Kiley's Run,
The sleepy river murmurs low,
And far away one dimly sees
Beyond the stretch of forest trees —
Beyond the foothills dusk and dun —
The ranges sleeping in the sun
  On Kiley's Run.

'Tis many years since first I came
  To Kiley's Run,
More years than I would care to name
Since I, a stripling, used to ride
For miles and miles at Kiley's side,
The while in stirring tones he told
The stories of the days of old
  On Kiley's Run.

I see the old bush homestead now
  On Kiley's Run,
Just nestled down beneath the brow
Of one small ridge above the sweep
Of river flat, where willows weep
And jasmine flowers and roses bloom,
The air was laden with perfume
  On Kiley's Run.

We lived the good old station life
  On Kiley's Run,
With little thought of care or strife.
Old Kiley seldom used to roam,
He liked to make the Run his home,
The swagman never turned away
With empty hand at close of day
  From Kiley's Run.

J. J. Hilder 1881–1916
Landscape near Carlingford. 1910
watercolour over pencil on wove paper on cardboard, 37.5 × 29.5 cm
from the collection of the Queensland Art Gallery

We kept a racehorse now and then
   On Kiley's Run,
And neighb'ring stations brought their men
To meetings where the sport was free
And dainty ladies came to see
Their champions ride; with laugh and song
The old house rang the whole night long
   On Kiley's Run.

The station hands were friends I wot
   On Kiley's Run,
A reckless, merry-hearted lot —
All splendid riders, and they knew
The "boss" was kindness through and through.
Old Kiley always stood their friend,
And so they served him to the end
   On Kiley's Run.

But droughts and losses came apace
   To Kiley's Run,
Till ruin stared him in the face;
He toiled and toiled while lived the light,
He dreamed of overdrafts at night:
At length, because he could not pay,
His bankers took the stock away
   From Kiley's Run.

Old Kiley stood and saw them go
   From Kiley's Run.
The well-bred cattle marching slow;
His stockmen, mates for many a day,
They wrung his hand and went away.
Too old to make another start,
Old Kiley died — of broken heart,
   On Kiley's Run.

The owner lives in England now
   Of Kiley's Run.
He knows a racehorse from a cow;
But that is all he knows of stock:
His chiefest care is how to dock
Expenses, and he sends from town
To cut the shearers' wages down
   On Kiley's Run.

There are no neighbours anywhere
   Near Kiley's Run.
The hospitable homes are bare,
The gardens gone; for no pretence
Must hinder cutting down expense:
The homestead that we held so dear
Contains a half-paid overseer
   On Kiley's Run.

All life and sport and hope have died
   On Kiley's Run.
No longer there the stockmen ride;
For sour-faced boundary riders creep
On mongrel horses after sheep,
Through ranges where, at racing speed,
Old Kiley used to "wheel the lead"
   On Kiley's Run.

There runs a lane for thirty miles
   Through Kiley's Run.
On either side the herbage smiles,
But wretched trav'lling sheep must pass
Without a drink or blade of grass
Thro' that long lane of death and shame:
The weary drovers curse the name
   Of Kiley's Run.

The name itself is changed of late
   Of Kiley's Run.
They call it "Chandos Park Estate".
The lonely swagman through the dark
Must hump his swag past Chandos Park.
The name is English, don't you see,
The old name sweeter sounds to me
   Of "Kiley's Run".

I cannot guess what fate will bring
   To Kiley's Run —
For chances come and changes ring —
I scarcely think 'twill always be
Locked up to suit an absentee;
And if he lets it out in farms
His tenants soon will carry arms
   On Kiley's Run.

Pioneers

They came of bold and roving stock that would not fixed abide;
They were the sons of field and flock since e'er they learned to ride;
We may not hope to see such men in these degenerate years
As those explorers of the bush — the brave old pioneers.

'Twas they who rode the trackless bush in heat and storm and drought;
'Twas they that heard the master-word that called them further out;
'Twas they that followed up the trail the mountain cattle made
And pressed across the mighty range where now their bones are laid.

But now the times are dull and slow, the brave old days are dead
When hardy bushmen started out, and forced their way ahead
By tangled scrub and forests grim towards the unknown west,
And spied the far-off promised land from off the ranges' crest.

Oh! ye, that sleep in lonely graves by far-off ridge and plain,
We drink to you in silence now as Christmas comes again,
The men who fought the wilderness through rough, unsettled years —
The founders of our nation's life, the brave old pioneers.

Margaret Preston
Flying over the Shoalhaven River. 1942
oil on canvas, 50.6 × 50.6 cm
collection: Australian National Gallery, Canberra

The Uplift

When the drays are bogged and sinking, then it's no use sitting thinking,
    You must put the teams together and must double-bank the pull.
When the crop is light and weedy, or the fleece is burred and seedy,
    Then the next year's crop and fleeces may repay you to the full.

    So it's lift her, Johnny, lift her,
    Put your back in it and shift her,
While the jabber, jabber, jabber of the politicians flows.
    If your nag's too poor to travel
    Then get down and scratch the gravel
For you'll get there if you walk it — if you don't, you'll feed the crows.

Shall we waste our time debating with a grand young country waiting
    For the plough and for the harrow and the lucerne and the maize?
For it's work alone will save us in the land that fortune gave us
    There's no crop but what we'll grow it; there's no stock but what we'll raise.

    When the team is bogged and sinking
    Then it's no use sitting thinking.
There's a roadway up the mountain that the old black leader knows:
    So it's lift her, Johnny, lift her,
    Put your back in it and shift her,
Take a lesson from the bullock — he goes slowly, but he goes!

Tom Roberts 1856–1931
Sherbrook Forest. 1924
oil on canvas, 48.3 × 68.6 cm
Art Gallery of New South Wales

Song of the Wheat

We have sung the song of the droving days,
　Of the march of the travelling sheep;
By silent stages and lonely ways
　Thin, white battalions creep.
But the man who now by the land would thrive
　Must his spurs to a ploughshare beat.
Is there ever a man in the world alive
　To sing the song of the Wheat!

It's west by south of the Great Divide
　The grim grey plains run out,
Where the old flock masters lived and died
　In a ceaseless fight with drought.
Weary with waiting and hope deferred
　They were ready to own defeat,
Till at last they heard the master-word
　And the master-word was Wheat.

Yarran and Myall and Box and Pine —
　'Twas axe and fire for all;
They scarce could tarry to blaze the line
　Or wait for the trees to fall,
Ere the team was yoked and the gates flung wide,
　And the dust of the horses' feet
Rose up like a pillar of smoke to guide
　The wonderful march of Wheat.

Furrow by furrow, and fold by fold,
　The soil is turned on the plain;
Better than silver and better than gold
　Is the surface-mine of the grain.
Better than cattle and better than sheep
　In the fight with the drought and heat.
For a streak of stubbornness wide and deep
　Lies hid in a grain of Wheat.

David Davies 1864–1939 Australian
Warm Evening, Templestowe
oil on canvas, 38.3 × 48.2 cm
Purchased with the assistance of a special grant
from the Government of Victoria, 1979
National Gallery of Victoria, Melbourne

When the stock is swept by the hand of fate,
    Deep down in his bed of clay
The brave brown Wheat will lie and wait
    For the resurrection day:
Lie hid while the whole world thinks him dead;
    But the spring rain, soft and sweet,
Will over the steaming paddocks spread
    The first green flush of the Wheat.

Green and amber and gold it grows
    When the sun sinks late in the west
And the breeze sweeps over the rippling rows
    Where the quail and the skylark nest.
Mountain or river or shining star,
    There's never a sight can beat —
Away to the skyline stretching far —
    A sea of the ripening Wheat.

When the burning harvest sun sinks low,
    And the shadows stretch on the plain,
The roaring strippers come and go
    Like ships on a sea of grain;
Till the lurching, groaning waggons bear
    Their tale of the load complete.
Of the world's great work he has done his share
    Who has gathered a crop of wheat.

Princes and Potentates and Czars,
    They revel in regal state,
But old King Wheat has a thousand cars
    For his trip to the water-gate;
And his thousand steamships breast the tide
    And plough thro' the wind and sleet
To the lands where the teeming millions bide
    That say, "Thank God for Wheat!"

60

In Defence of the Bush

So you're back from up the country, Mister Lawson, where you went,
And you're cursing all the business in a bitter discontent;
Well, we grieve to disappoint you, and it makes us sad to hear
That it wasn't cool and shady — and there wasn't plenty beer,
And the loony bullock snorted when you first came into view;
Well, you know it's not so often that he sees a swell like you;
And the roads were hot and dusty, and the plains were burnt and brown,
And no doubt you're better suited drinking lemon squash in town.

Yet, perchance, if you should journey down the very track you went
In a month or two at furthest you would wonder what it meant,
Where the sunbaked earth was gasping like a creature in its pain
You would find the grasses waving like a field of summer grain,
And the miles of thirsty gutters blocked with sand and choked with mud,
You would find them mighty rivers with a turbid, sweeping flood;
For the rain and drought and sunshine make no changes in the street,
In the sullen line of buildings and the ceaseless tramp of feet;
But the bush hath moods and changes, as the seasons rise and fall,
And the men who know the bush land — they are loyal through it all.

But you found the bush was dismal and a land of no delight,
Did you chance to hear a chorus in the shearers' huts at night?
Did they "rise up, William Riley" by the camp-fire's cheery blaze?
Did they rise him as we rose him in the good old droving days?
And the women of the homesteads and the men you chanced to meet —
Were their faces sour and saddened like the "faces in the street",
And the "shy selector children" — were they better now or worse
Than the little city urchins who would greet you with a curse?
Is not such a life much better than the squalid street and square
Where the fallen women flaunt it in the fierce electric glare,
Where the semptress plies her sewing till her eyes are sore and red
In a filthy, dirty attic toiling on for daily bread?
Did you hear no sweeter voices in the music of the bush
Than the roar of trams and buses, and the war whoop of "the push"?
Did the magpies rouse your slumbers with their carol sweet and strange?

Did you hear the silver chiming of the bellbirds on the range?
But, perchance, the wild birds' music by your senses was despised,
For you say you'll stay in townships till the bush is civilised.
Would you make it a tea garden and on Sundays have a band
Where the "blokes" might take their "donahs", with a "public" close at hand?
You had better stick to Sydney and make merry with the "push",
For the bush will never suit you, and you'll never suit the bush.

Index of Poems

Index of Plates

Index of First Lines